Introducing

AYRSHIRE
& ARRAN

Jack Forrest

**with photographs by
Dennis Hardley**

land o' Burns

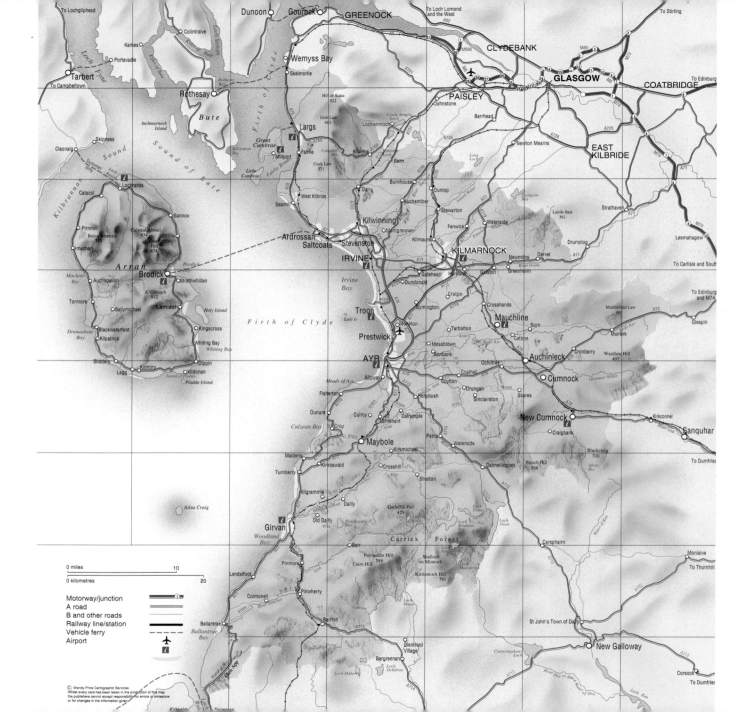

Legend:
- Motorway/junction
- A road
- B and other roads
- Railway line/station
- Vehicle ferry
- Airport

0 miles 10
0 kilometres 20

© Wendy Price Cartographic Services
Whilst every care has been taken in the production of this map
the publishers cannot accept responsibility for errors or omissions
or for changes in the information given.

INTRODUCING
Ayrshire and Arran land o' Burns

Lush, fertile undulating hills, craggy mountains reaching down to the sea, castles and monuments, seaside towns and quiet country retreats – they are all within reach in the extensive holiday area of Ayrshire and Arran.

Many castles in Ayrshire are more than 400 years old. Most of the earlier fortified stockades were built by Anglo-French warriors in support of Scottish Kings. The later examples of finely proportioned stone castles, were built in times of family feuding when necessity demanded strong structures.

Ayrshire is also noted for its place in shaping Scotland's industrial might. The area held many natural resources; water to power mills, coal to feed engines and iron to forge machines. The population grew during the industrial revolution and the lives of many folk changed. An array of visitor centres and museums throughout the area mark these changes and the effect they had on the people and towns.

The coast of Ayrshire boasts several championship golf courses. Skelmorlie to Girvan is almost a network of links courses where great stretches of rolling greens offer challenges for every standard of golfer. Ayrshire has some thirty seven golf courses and the effect of the Gulf Stream means lovely springy turf, great dipping hollows and awesome bunkers – all with splendid vistas and breathtaking views.

With over eighty miles of Scotland's south-western coastline, more than twenty lochs and reservoirs, and as many rivers to enjoy, the Arran and Ayrshire area also offers a feast of activity in the great sport of fishing to suit all tastes and talents. Information is always available locally on where to charter boats or gear or obtain permits.

Our journey starts in the south of Ayrshire where Ailsa Craig, the spectacular granite mass rising out of the sea, is visible from all aspects of this lovely coastline. The rock, and its colony of gannets, can be reached by a boat trip from the harbour at Girvan.

Set high on a clifftop near the village of Maybole is Robert Adam's masterpiece, Culzean Castle. Cared for by

Opposite: Ailsa Craig rises 339 metres above the Firth of Clyde, 10 miles offshore from Girvan. Also known as Paddy's Milestone, this micro-granite mass used to be quarried for curling stones.

the National Trust for Scotland, this beautiful building and its gardens, said to be the most magnificent country park in Britain, are well worth visiting. En route we will have passed Turnberry, birthplace of Robert the Bruce. Little remains today of Turnberry Castle which was the meeting place of supporters of Bruce's claim to the Scottish throne. More recently of course, Turnberry received acclaim as the first purpose-built golf resort in Scotland.

Above and left: Girvan has been a popular holiday destination since the arrival of the railway in 1860. Originally a village where herring fishing and handloom weaving were the main occupations, the town today boasts many facilities and a fine harbour with splendid views out to sea.

Set among sand dunes along a spectacular shore, the club was founded in 1902 and its impressive first-class hotel was built by the Glasgow and South-West Railway in 1904.

The town of Ayr is very ancient and it is known that communities have lived, and worked the land there, for eight hundred years.

Above and right: *The magnificent Turnberry Hotel was originally built in 1904 and Turnberry Lighthouse which is a landmark of the links courses is a prominent navigation light on the Clyde.*

Standing at the mouth of the river of the same name, the town grew up as an important seaport where woollens, fish, salt and coal were exported, and goods such as wine, spices, fruit, timber and wax were imported from France, Norway and the Baltic. But it was in the 1830s, with the arrival of the railway, that Ayr became the famous holiday destination it is today. Glasgow folk discovered that

Opposite: *Turnberry was the first purpose-built golf resort in Scotland and today boasts two world class championship courses. During both world wars the links were used for military airfields.*

Ayr's beaches were within reasonable travelling distance and holiday-makers flocked to the coast.

In the town itself, the old blends comfortably with the new. The Ayr "Auld Brig" which was constructed in the 15th century, and gained fame through Burns' poem "The Brigs of Ayr", was carefully restored in 1907. Judge for yourself how this delightful ancient fixture contrasts with the more modern Ayr New Bridge or whether Burns' words are correct:

Opposite and above: *The strategic position of Culzean Castle was recognised by the Kennedy family in the 12th century. Today's Culzean Castle was commissioned by David Kennedy, the 10th Earl of Cassilis. Robert Adam was responsible for the castle's ambitious design. Building was completed by the end of the 18th century. Now in the care of the National Trust for Scotland, the castle's beautiful walled gardens, deer park, swan pond and aviary certainly justify a visit.*

"buskit in a braw new coat, that he, at Lo'on, frae ane Adams got, pours scorn on the Auld"

The new bridge which Burns scorns was in fact designed by Robert Adam and built in 1788. It was destroyed by a flood and replaced by the existing five arched New Brig in 1877.

Today modern Ayr stretches south to the river Doon and encompasses the village of Alloway, birthplace of Scotland's National poet, Robert Burns.

Born on the 25th January 1759, Robert Burns spent the first seven years of his childhood in this village where his father, a market gardener and fairly unsuccessful tenant farmer, encouraged his son in the art of "penmanship." By his mid-twenties Burns was an accomplished poet and songwriter and in 1786 he published his famous Kilmarnock edition of poems. Burns enjoyed life to the full and most of all he enjoyed falling in love. His works include hundreds of love songs – the two best known being of course, (My Love Is Like) "A Red, Red Rose" and "Ae Fond Kiss." Now famed the world over, Burns' poetry has been translated into

Right: *A view of the loch and boat house in the gardens at Bargany House, an Ayrshire mansion dating back to 1681.*

Opposite: *The ruins of 13th century Crossraguel Abbey, in the care of Historic Scotland. In 1404 a royal charter gave the monks the privilege to mint their own coins and brew ale.*

many languages and his life is remembered in a variety of visitor attractions on the Burns Heritage Trail which weaves its way through Ayrshire.

Further north, the towns of Prestwick and Troon, also famed for their golf courses, offer many other delights such as a large indoor bowling stadium, another pastime for which Ayrshire is famed, windsurfing and go-karting. The marina at Troon provides shelter for yachtsmen, and its award-winning beach is a great draw for the family.

Travelling east takes us inward and the delights of towns such as Kilmarnock and Mauchline. There is certainly plenty to explore in Dean Castle at Kilmarnock where the dungeons and battlements vie with the

Above: *Dunure Castle stands prominently against the sea. This view looks north up the Ayrshire coast.*

Opposite: *Doon Castle near Dalmellington once stood upon an island but was moved to the loch shore in the 1930s when the level of the loch was raised for a hydro-electric scheme.*

lovely tapestries and amazing mediaeval armour. The town's Galleon Centre has much to offer in the way of sports facilities and at Loudoun Castle Park, Galston, you will find an amazing combination of castle ruins, fairground and woodland walks.

History is everywhere in east Ayrshire; Burns is remembered in Mauchline and further on is the magnificent

14th century Sorn Castle which sits overlooking the River Ayr. The ancient town of Cumnock is here too. The area around the Doon Valley used to resound to the clatter of weaving shuttles and coal and iron production. There are still echoes from that past at the Ironworks museum and the Scottish Industrial Railway Centre.

North Ayrshire with its panoramic views across to

An atmospheric photograph of Ayr with the New Bridge, built in 1877, spanning the River Ayr.

Above: *Time to relax in Ayr's Wellington Square.*

Left: *An upstream view of the River Ayr with a wide variety of birds feeding in the tidal part of the river.*

Great Cumbrae and the Isle of Arran, is an area of great discovery. Largs is a very fine seaside town with a splendid promenade and marina, a far cry from 1263 when the town resounded to cries and cheers as the Vikings were driven home after Scotland's last great Viking battle. At Vikingar you can join in the re-enactment of that battle and the drama of life in Viking times. Other warriors have also had success in Ayrshire – William Wallace defeated the English at Loudoun Hill in 1297 and Robert the Bruce, the most famous of all Scottish Kings repeated this success ten years later.

It is supposed that the name of "Largs" is derived from the Gaelic "Learg" meaning green slope and this town certainly reflects that name with its impressive spread of woodland and hills which rise grandly behind it.

Names have been carried from Largs to far afield – the city of Brisbane in Australia is named after General Sir Thomas MacDougall Brisbane who was born in Brisbane Glen in 1783.

Like Ayr, Largs has been a favourite holiday destination since the railways arrived and its safe, sheltered waters, and traditional seaside features, including world-renowned ice-cream, ensure that popularity continues today.

A panoramic view across Lamlash Bay, Arran, with Goat Fell (874m) in the distance.

Robert Burns *was born in Alloway on 25th January, 1759. Burns' Cottage, arguably the most famous cottage in the world, was built by Burns' father in 1757. Pictured above, the cottage now stands in its original size and condition having been restored in 1881 by the Trustees of Burns Monument Trust. It was here Burns lived for the first seven years of his life.*

Opposite: *The* **Burns Monument** *stands proudly by the banks of the River Doon and was opened to the public in 1823. Today a holiday in Scotland would not be complete without visiting Alloway and the Burns National Heritage Park including* **The Tam o' Shanter Experience.**

The towns along the north of Ayrshire's coastline continue to tell the story of the area's part in history. Irvine is a new town with a distinctly strong feel of the past. Glasgow Vennel, a delightful cobbled street in the town, was once the main road to Glasgow. Seagate Castle was already ancient when Mary Queen of Scots stayed there in 1563.

Above: *A view across the Largs Channel towards Great Cumbrae from Routenburn Golf Club.*

Opposite: *Irvine harbour is home to the Scottish Maritime Museum. The Magnum Centre in Irvine is the largest indoor and outdoor recreational complex in Scotland.*

Right: *Boarding the ferry at Great Cumbrae, location of Scotland's National Watersport Centre.*

The "Three Towns" of Ardrossan, Saltcoats and Stevenson are set around a sheltered bay north of Irvine. Saltcoats grew out of the salt-panning industry and Stevenson, where the first safe explosive was made are well worth exploring. Inland you will find not only further evidence of history in Dalry, Kilbirnie and Beith, but an abundance of walking and fishing opportunities.

We continue to the port of Ardrossan, whose 12th century castle was ransacked by Oliver Cromwell. This is your starting point for the hour long journey to the beautiful Isle of Arran. Sometimes called "Scotland in Miniature" and meaning "peaked island" in Gaelic, one thing is certain – time spent

Right: *A colourful view of Largs from the sea. Largs is a popular seaside resort and the paddle steamer Waverley offers day excursions 'doon the watter' when passengers can enjoy the skirl of the pipes and the embracing sea air.*

Opposite: *A superb view above Largs and over the Firth of Clyde to Bute and Argyll.*

on Arran will never be forgotten. The Firth of Clyde's largest island offers mountains, glens, moors and woodland, undulating lowland hills and, wherever you go, you will never be far from its splendid seascape. Whether you want to cycle, pony trek, golf, sail or fish, or allow yourself to fall into step with the slower pace of the island and walk along quiet shores

Opposite: *A view from the esplanade at Millport, Isle of Cumbrae. Millport's Cathedral of the Isles, is the smallest cathedral in Britain.*

or tree-lined tracks Arran is for you.

The north of Arran is a fairly rough and mountainous area where its highest hill, Goat Fell (874m) and neighbouring peaks of Beinn Bhreac and Beinn Tarsuinn are to be found. These unmistakable landmarks are visible from a wide area of western Scotland and once seen silhouetted against the sunset, will remain in the memory forever. To the south the landscape is more gentle

Above: *The ferry from Brodick on the Isle of Arran departs for Ardrossan.*

Below: *The picturesque village of Lamlash on Arran.*

Above: *An early morning view across Brodick Bay towards Brodick Castle and right, the beautiful gardens of Brodick Castle.*

and offers fine seascapes down the Firth of Clyde over Pladda Island. The secret of Arran's geology unfolded in the late nineteenth century and the island remains a popular destination for university field trips.

The main town of Brodick (meaning "broad bay" in Norse) has many hotels, guest houses and shops and is also the starting point for many trips round this lovely

Opposite: *Brodick Castle's early history began in 1503 and has continued with demolitions, rebuilding and subsequent additions throughout the centuries. The property now belongs to the National Trust for Scotland.*

island. Brodick Castle at the north of the bay was once a residence of the Dukes of Hamilton and is now in the care of the National Trust for Scotland which also owns the spectacular Glen Rosa and Goat Fell. Heading south the first village encountered is Lamlash which lies sheltered behind the bulk of Holy Island. Lamlash and the nearby village of Whiting Bay have many guest houses and attractions for tourists but as

we continue our journey to the south of Arran, we enter a more Hebridean world of small crofting townships, panoramic coastlines and peace.

The road meanders through an array of villages with beautiful names and appearances to the picturesque harbour of Blackwaterfoot on Arran's west coast. Much of this area is best known for its prehistoric and geological attractions. Standing stones,

The quiet and picturesque village of Corrie and **right**, *a view up Glen Sannox.*

Opposite: *The shoreline at Corrie looking north, up the Clyde estuary.*

stone circles and hut circles are a reminder that four thousand years ago this was one of the most important ritual landscapes in Bronze Age Britain.

On the north-west of the island is the village of Lochranza with its ancient castle. During the summer months there is a short ferry route from Lochranza to the north-east coast of Kintyre.

Arran has a wealth of history, geology and scenery for its visitors to enjoy and it truly lives up to its reputation as "Scotland in Miniature".

The Ayrshire and Arran area boasts a superb selection of impressive gardens and woodlands to explore. The vast grounds of Culzean Castle and the delightful gardens at Brodick Castle have already been mentioned but the list continues with Kelburn Country Park with its colourful displays, two hundred acres of prime woodland at Dean Castle,

Above: *An unusual perspective on Loch Ranza Castle on the north of Arran.*

Right: *Leaving Lochranza for Claonaig on the Campbeltown peninsula.*

the peaceful grounds of
Blairquhan Castle which
open in the summer and the
azaleas and rhododendrons
of Bargany should not be
missed. Many other private
gardens open under
"Scotland's Garden Scheme"
(look for the yellow signs)
give the opportunity to

Right: *The isle of Pladda with Ailsa Craig on the horizon, seen from Arran's south coast.*

Opposite: *A dramatic 'contre jour' shot of the mountains on Arran seen from the Kilbrannan Sound.*

explore grounds not usually open to the public.

Wherever you stay on your journey around Ayrshire and Arran you will be assured of a warm welcome with a wide selection of accommodation from which to choose. Whether you are after an action-packed holiday with a great choice of sports activities, or a leisurely break to take in the contrasting scenery and browse round some of Scotland's history, you are sure to want to return again to this lovely corner of Scotland.

Right: *A beautiful sunset across the sea towards Arran from Prestwick.*

Ayrshire and Arran Tourist Board – Tourist Information Centres

AYR: Burns House, Burns Statue Square.
Tel: 01292 288688
BRODICK: The Pier, Isle of Arran.
Tel: 01770 302140/302401
IRVINE: New Street.
Tel: 01294 313886
KILMARNOCK: 62 Bank Street.
Tel: 01563 539090
LARGS: The Promenade.
Tel: 01475 673765

MAUCHLINE: Burns Memorial Tower,
Kilmarnock Rd. Tel: 01290 551916
GIRVAN: Bridge Street.
Tel: 01465 714950
TROON: South Beach.
Tel: 01292 317696
MILLPORT: 28 Stuart Street, Isle of Cumbrae.
Tel: 01475 530753

A TIC is also located at the Ardrossan/Brodick Ferry

Ayrshire
&Arran
TOURIST BOARD